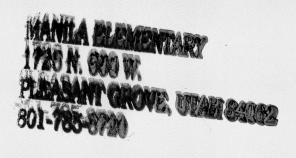

FIRST TIME IN A SWIMMING POOL.

SKATEBOARDING CAT!

T.J.'S FAVORITE BALL.

DRAGGING BOOTS AROUND IS TIRING.

POSING FOR THE CAMERA.

T.J. BLENDS IN WITH LEAVES AND GRASS WHEN HE HIDES.

TIGER MATH

LEARNING TO GRAPH FROM A BABY TIGER

BY ANN WHITEHEAD NAGDA

AND CINDY BICKEL

Henry Holt and Company

New York

For my father—A. W. N.
For Steve, my husband—C. B.

Henry Holt and Company, LLC
Publishers since 1866
175 Fifth Avenue
New York, New York 10010
www.HenryHoltKids.com

Library of Congress Cataloging-in-Publication Data
Nagda, Ann Whitehead.
Tiger math: learning to graph from a baby tiger / by Ann Whitehead Nagda and Cindy Bickel.
Summary: Describes by means of words and graphs the growth of an orphan Siberian tiger cub.
1. Graphic methods—Juvenile literature. 2. Tigers—Juvenile literature.
[1. Graphic methods. 2. Tigers. 3. Animals—Infancy.]
I. Bickel, Cindy. II. Title.
QA90.N26 2000 511'.5—dc21 99-46686

ISBN-13: 978-0-8050-6248-9 / ISBN-10: 0-8050-6248-3 (hardcover)
7 9 10 8 6

ISBN-13: 978-0-8050-7161-0 / ISBN-10: 0-8050-7161-X (paperback)
7 9 10 8 6

First published in hardcover by Henry Holt and Company
First paperback edition—2002
Printed in the United States of America on acid-free paper. ∞

We are grateful for the cooperation of the Denver Zoo, Denver, Colorado.

HOW MANY BALLS CAN ONE TIGER CUB DESTROY? AS MANY AS YOU GIVE HIM.

T.J., THE BABY TIGER.

INTRODUCTION

It is a very special event when a Siberian tiger is born, because there are so few of them left in the world. This book will use graphs to help tell the story of T.J., a Siberian tiger cub born at the Denver Zoo. Just as words can tell a story, so can graphs. Graphs are math pictures that make it easy to see and understand information about numbers. This book will introduce four different kinds of graphs: picture graphs, circle graphs, bar graphs, and line graphs. If you want to read the story of T.J. the tiger without the math, you can read only the right-hand pages of this book. Then to learn more and see exactly how T.J. grew, you can look at the graphs on the left-hand pages.

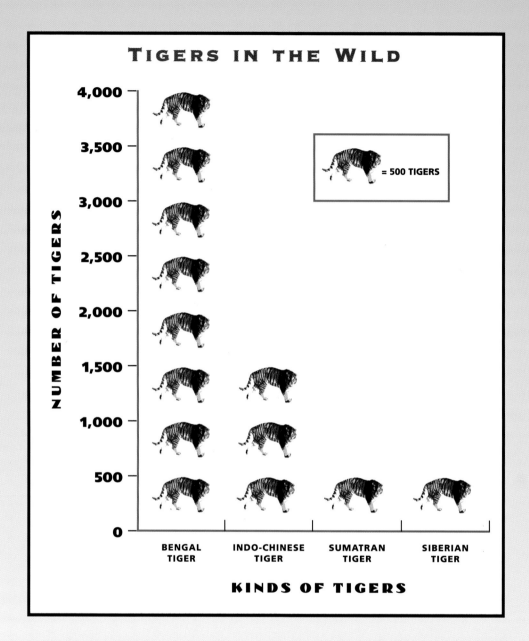

TIGERS IN THE WILD

NUMBER OF TIGERS

4,000
3,500
3,000
2,500
2,000
1,500
1,000
500
0

= 500 TIGERS

BENGAL TIGER · INDO-CHINESE TIGER · SUMATRAN TIGER · SIBERIAN TIGER

KINDS OF TIGERS

Picture graphs use pictures to make it easy to compare things. The image above is a picture graph that shows how many tigers are left in the wild. Each tiger drawing stands for 500 tigers. To read this graph, choose a kind of tiger from the names along the bottom. Then count how many tiger drawings are in that tiger's column and multiply that number by 500. This graph makes it easy to see that there are fewer Sumatran and Siberian tigers than there are other kinds of tigers.

T.J., THE TIGER CUB, AND BUHKRA, HIS MOTHER.

Buhkra, the Siberian tiger, was going to have a baby. The keepers at the Denver Zoo had already placed a video camera in her den, so they could check on the mother tiger without disturbing her. When the cub was born, they watched Buhkra and her baby on a TV screen. Buhkra was a good mother, licking, nuzzling, and nursing her new baby. The cub, named T.J., weighed only three pounds and looked tiny next to his mother, who weighed 250 pounds. T.J.'s father, Matthew, was even bigger than Buhkra. He weighed 350 pounds. T.J. would have to gain a lot of weight to be as big as his father.

TIGERS IN THE WILD

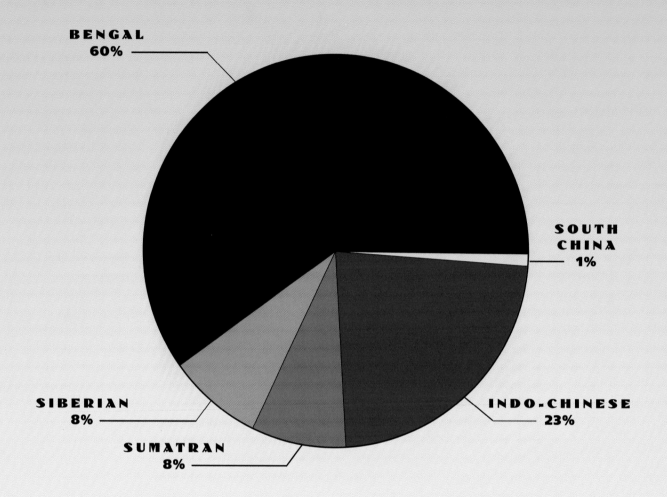

BENGAL 60%

SOUTH CHINA 1%

INDO-CHINESE 23%

SIBERIAN 8%

SUMATRAN 8%

Another way to show how many tigers are left in the wild is to use a circle graph. A circle graph, or pie chart, shows what part of a whole something is. The whole circle represents all the tigers left in the world. This graph makes it easy to see that there are a lot of Bengal tigers and very few South China tigers. There are so few South China tigers left that they couldn't be shown on the picture graph on page 8—they would have been just a small piece of a tiger picture.

MATTHEW, T.J.'S FATHER, WEIGHS 350 POUNDS.

When T.J. was six weeks old, the zoo veterinarian gave him shots and weighed him. The cub weighed ten pounds. When T.J.'s father was six weeks old, he weighed fourteen pounds, four pounds more than T.J. Even so, the little tiger was healthy and strong. Sheila, the tiger keeper, had trouble holding him still while the vet examined him. The feisty little cub never stopped wriggling until Sheila brought him back to his mother.

11

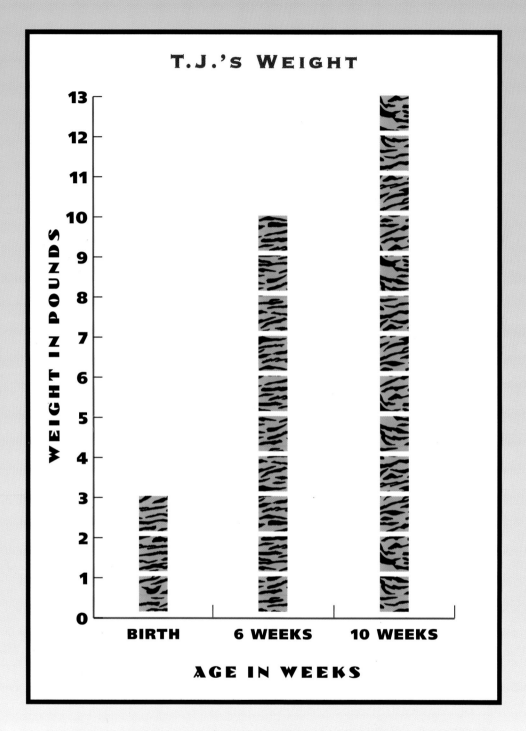

A picture graph can be used to show T.J.'s weight. This is a picture graph like the one on page 8. On this graph, blocks are used instead of pictures of tigers. Each block is equal to one pound. Each column shows T.J.'s weight at a particular age.

T.J., THE TIGER CUB.

Every day when Sheila came to the zoo, the first thing she did was check on the tigers. Buhkra, protecting her cub, always snarled, spit, and bared her teeth at Sheila. T.J. snarled just like his mother.

One morning, Buhkra didn't snarl at Sheila. The mother tiger lay on her side, completely still. T.J. was mewing and pushing his mother and trying to nurse, but Buhkra didn't move. Without any warning, she had died. The zoo veterinarian examined Buhkra and discovered she'd died from cancer.

Now who would raise this special baby? Most of the time, mother tigers take care of their cubs alone. Matthew couldn't take care of his son—he didn't know how.

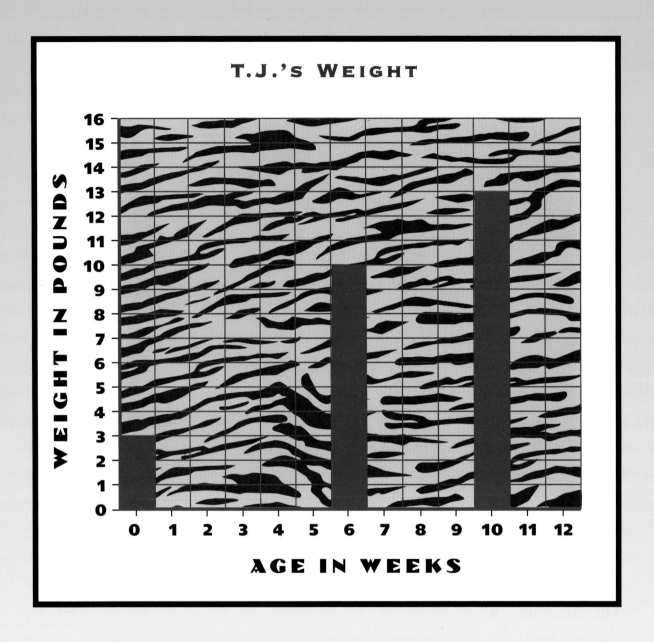

T.J.'S WEIGHT

Another way to graph T.J.'s weight is with a bar graph. This bar graph of T.J.'s weight looks a lot like the picture graph. Each colored square equals one pound, just like the blocks in the picture graph. To read the bar graph, choose an age from the numbers along the bottom. Then follow the colored bar up until it stops at a line. Follow that line to the left to find out how much T.J. weighed at the age you have chosen.

Sheila took T.J. to be raised by the staff at the animal hospital. The vet was worried when he examined the cub. T.J. was not as big as he should have been. The cub was ten weeks old and he weighed only thirteen pounds. Because Buhkra had been sick, she hadn't been able to feed her cub enough.

Cindy, a veterinary assistant at the hospital, put T.J. in a cage and gave him a bowl of ground meat mixed with milk. Ignoring the food, T.J. walked to a corner of the cage, curled into a ball, and didn't move for hours. The next day he was still curled up in the same spot. He hadn't touched his food.

The hospital staff was worried. The ten-week-old cub hadn't gained much weight since his six-week checkup. If he didn't start eating soon, he would lose weight, which would be bad for his health.

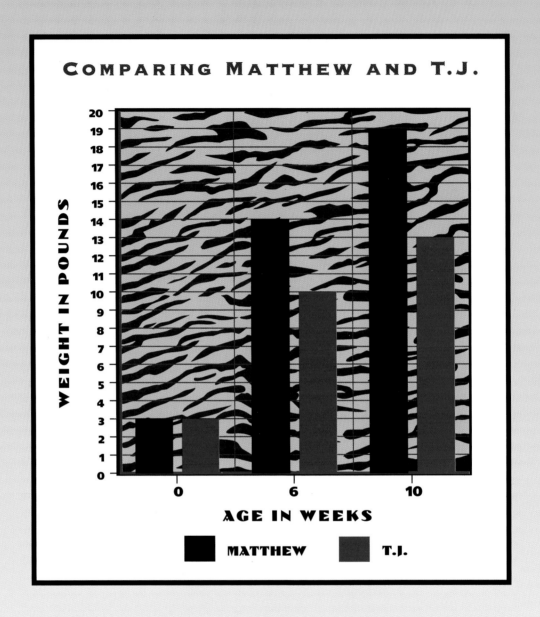

COMPARING MATTHEW AND T.J.

WEIGHT IN POUNDS

AGE IN WEEKS

MATTHEW   T.J.

The vet checked to see how much T.J.'s father had weighed as a cub. He compared T.J.'s weight with Matthew's weight at the same ages. At six weeks, Matthew weighed four pounds more than T.J. At ten weeks, Matthew weighed six pounds more than T.J.

Cindy made a bar graph like this one to compare the tigers' weights. The red bars show T.J.'s weight. The black bars show Matthew's weight. This graph makes it easy to see that although Matthew and T.J. weighed the same amount at birth, Matthew gained more weight than his son did in a ten-week period.

T.J. FLATTENS HIS EARS AND SNARLS WHEN HE IS FRIGHTENED.

It was T.J.'s third day at the hospital and he still hadn't eaten. When Cindy entered his cage, he snarled and showed his teeth, threatening her because he was scared. She put some meat on a wooden stick and placed the meat in his mouth. T.J. spat it out.

The next day Cindy tried giving him strained meat from a jar. She thought that T.J. might like human baby food. He spat that out too.

CINDY MAKES A LINE GRAPH OF T.J.'S WEIGHT.

Cindy used the zoo's computer to make a line graph of T.J.'s weight like the one below. Line graphs make it easy to see how something changes. This line graph shows how T.J.'s weight changed as he grew older. Each point on the graph shows how much T.J. weighed at a certain age. The line that connects the points makes it easier to see the whole story that the graph tells.

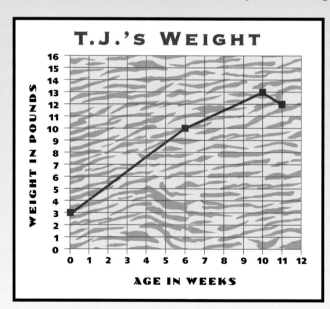

Cindy's graph told a disappointing story. T.J. was losing weight. The tiger cub had lost one pound during his first few days in the hospital.

HOW MANY PEOPLE DOES IT TAKE TO FEED ONE SMALL TIGER?
THREE. DR. CAMBRE AND DR. KENNY HOLD THE TIGER STILL
WHILE CINDY PUTS MEATBALLS IN HIS MOUTH.

Cindy and the staff began to fear for T.J.'s life. Five days had passed and the tiny cub had not eaten anything. Everyone agreed that they had no choice but to force T.J. to eat. Dr. Kenny and Dr. Cambre, wearing jackets and heavy gloves, held T.J. still while Cindy used a stick to place meat at the back of his tongue. It was quite a struggle at first—the small tiger was all teeth and claws. Finally T.J. swallowed seven meatballs coated with dried milk.

Cindy hoped that T.J. would eat on his own after he got a taste of food. But the cub still refused to touch the meat in his bowl. To help T.J. survive, Cindy and the veterinarians continued to force T.J. to eat.

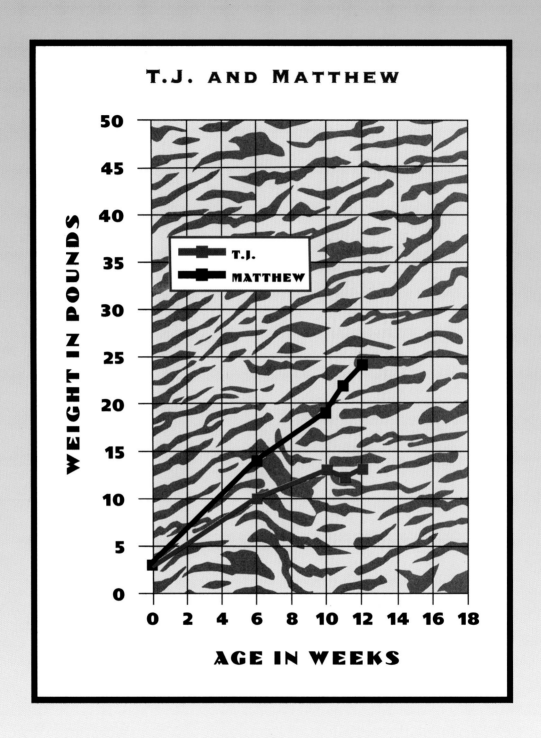

T.J. AND MATTHEW

Here is a line graph of both T.J.'s and Matthew's weight from birth to twelve weeks. The red line is T.J.'s weight. The black line is Matthew's weight. At twelve weeks, T.J. weighed a lot less than his father did at the same age.

T.J. ACCEPTS FOOD FROM CINDY.

On the eleventh day, T.J. ate two meatballs on his own. When Cindy gave the cub a rubber toy, he batted it around. Then she set a meaty bone next to the toy. T.J. immediately started chewing on the bone. Everyone started to feel more hopeful.

For a few days, T.J. seemed to be feeling better. He ate whatever Cindy gave him. Then suddenly he got fussy. When Cindy put a meatball in his mouth, he spat it out. He smashed the rest of the meatballs and buried them in the hay. To keep his weight up, the hospital staff forced the cub to eat again.

All the care and hard work paid off. T.J. gained weight at last.

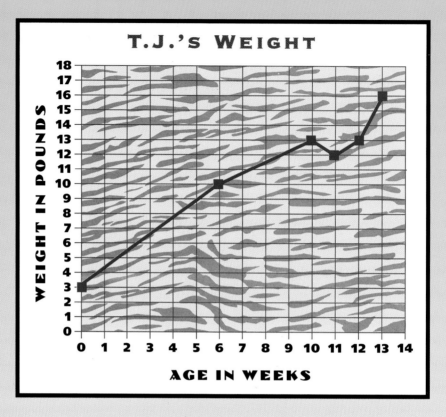

T.J.'S WEIGHT

WEIGHT IN POUNDS

AGE IN WEEKS

CINDY WEIGHS HERSELF
AND T.J.

Now the graph told a more hopeful story. Looking at the line graph, Cindy could see that T.J. had gained one pound between eleven and twelve weeks and three more pounds by thirteen weeks.

T.J. was weighed frequently. By thirteen weeks of age, the frisky cub was not cooperative about getting on a scale by himself. Cindy had to hold the tiger and step onto the scale. Together, Cindy and T.J. weighed 126 pounds. Cindy put the tiger down and stepped back onto the scale alone. It read 110 pounds. By subtracting her weight from their combined weight, Cindy was able to figure out that the tiger cub now weighed 16 pounds.

T.J. IS VERY EAGER TO EAT HIS MEAT.

Cindy was relieved when the tiger cub let her hand-feed him on a regular basis. Now he would gain weight more quickly. T.J.'s favorite food was beef heart rolled in dried milk. By the time he was fourteen weeks old, he weighed nineteen pounds. The cub was gaining weight at a steady rate, and the vet was pleased with his progress.

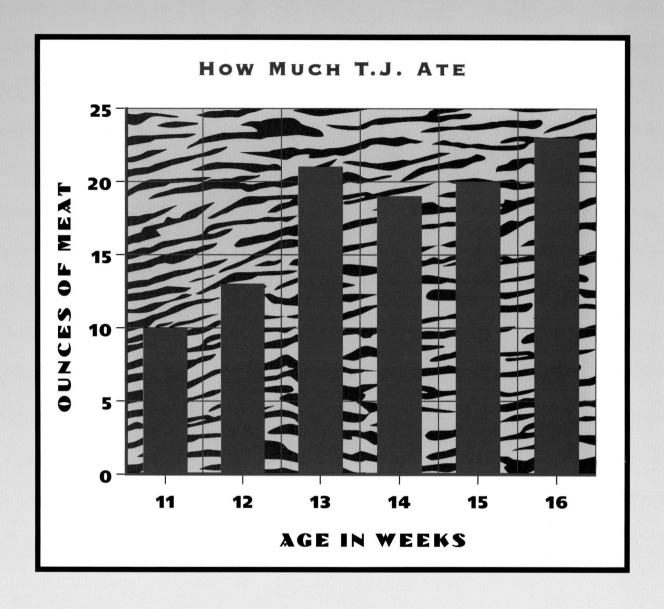

HOW MUCH T.J. ATE

Y-axis: OUNCES OF MEAT (0, 5, 10, 15, 20, 25)

X-axis: AGE IN WEEKS (11, 12, 13, 14, 15, 16)

This bar graph shows how much meat T.J. ate each day during his first weeks at the hospital. At eleven weeks, T.J. got very upset if he was forced to swallow more than ten ounces of meat a day. By thirteen weeks, the cub was eating a lot more. As his appetite increased, so did his weight.

HOW FAST CAN A TIGER LEARN
TO OPEN A REFRIGERATOR?

VERY FAST.
WHAT'S FOR DINNER?

As T.J. grew more comfortable with the nursery staff, he became more playful. He played hide-and-seek with Cindy and Denny, another veterinary assistant, on the zoo grounds at night. The tiger cub would hide in the bushes and wait patiently until Denny got close to him. Then he would leap out, grabbing Denny's leg with his paws. Sometimes he would sneak up behind Cindy and pounce on her. Tiger mothers teach their babies how to hunt by playing games like this.

The tiger quickly learned to open the nursery room door, so he could join his human friends in the kitchen. He also learned to open the refrigerator door by pulling on the towel hanging there. One time T.J. even helped himself to a bag of meat. By the end of T.J.'s stay in the zoo hospital, he wanted company all the time and cried when he was by himself.

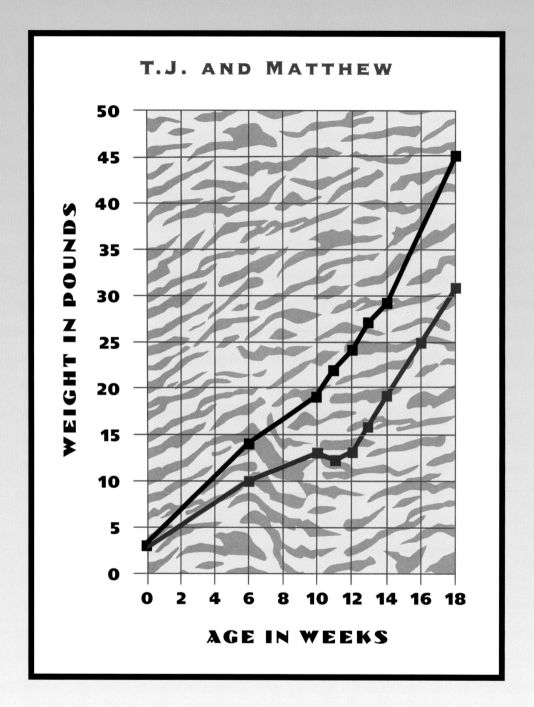

T.J. AND MATTHEW

WEIGHT IN POUNDS

AGE IN WEEKS

This line graph shows how the two tigers grew. When T.J. was eighteen weeks old, he weighed thirty-one pounds. At the same age, Matthew had weighed forty-five pounds. T.J. still had a way to go before he weighed as much as his father, but he was making progress.

SHEILA FEEDS T.J. T.J. SCRATCHES A TREE TRUNK.

After learning to live with humans, T.J. had a new challenge. He had to leave the hospital, return to the tiger exhibit in the zoo, and live by himself. Cindy visited him often. Sheila, the tiger keeper, hand-fed him so that he would get to know her. T.J. played games with Sheila. Sometimes he climbed on a rock and then pounced on her when she entered the exhibit.

T.J. was afraid to go outside in the tiger yard at first, so Sheila and Cindy went with him. Soon he was having a wonderful time, shredding bark from trees and watching birds and zoo visitors.

During the next few years, T.J. grew a lot.

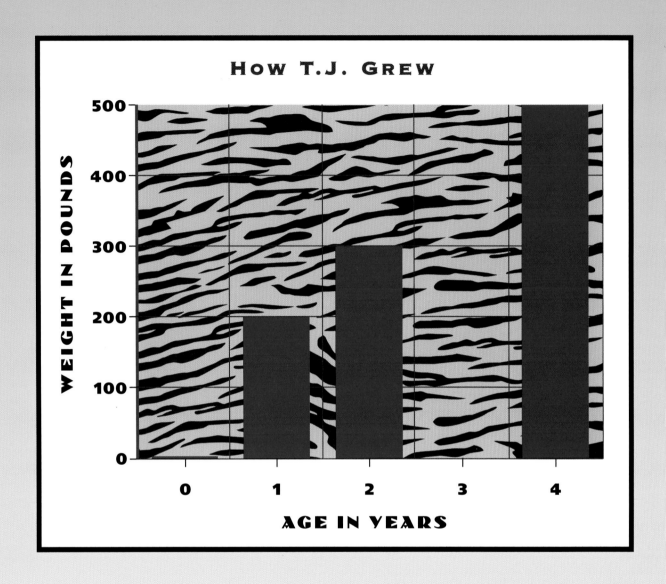

HOW T.J. GREW

WEIGHT IN POUNDS

AGE IN YEARS

This is a bar graph of how much weight T.J. gained from birth to four years old. T.J. may have gained weight very slowly just after his mother died, but by the time he was one year old, he had gained nearly 200 pounds. And by the time he was four, he weighed a healthy 500 pounds (even more than his father did). The graph finally tells a happy story.

T.J. SITS IN HIS POOL AT ZOOMONTANA.

When T.J. was two years old, he was moved to a zoo in Billings, Montana, where they had a brand-new tiger exhibit, but no tigers. T.J. was just what they needed (a big, sleek, healthy tiger, weighing 300 pounds). He continued to thrive in his new home.

Several years later when T.J. was four years old, Cindy went to visit him at ZooMontana. She watched the tiger splash around in his pool. After she called to him, T.J. came over to the fence and chuffled, which is a sound that tigers use as a greeting. Normally tigers chuffle only to each other, but if a tiger in captivity is especially fond of a person, he will chuffle when this favored person approaches. Cindy knew that T.J. still remembered her.

Cindy was amazed to see how big T.J. was. The tiger keeper at ZooMontana estimated that T.J. weighed 500 pounds. T.J. had finally grown bigger than his father!

HIDING AT THE HOSPITAL.

POUNCING ON CINDY.

HIDE-AND-SEEK WITH DENNY.

T.J. AT ZOOMONTANA.

RESTING ON THE ROCKS.